The Berkshire
YEOMANRY

200 Years of
Yeoman Service

Anthony Verey

Stuart Sampson

Andrew French

Simon Frost

ALAN SUTTON PUBLISHING LIMITED

First published in the United Kingdom in 1994 by
Alan Sutton Publishing Ltd · Phoenix Mill
Far Thrupp · Stroud · Gloucestershire

First published in the United States of America in 1994 by
Alan Sutton Inc. · 83 Washington Street · Dover
NH 03820

British Library Cataloguing in Publication Data

A catalogue record for this book is available from the
British Library.

ISBN 0-7509-0754-1

Library of Congress Cataloging in Publication Data
applied for

Typeset in 11/16 Palatino.
Typesetting and origination by
Alan Sutton Publishing Limited.
Printed in Great Britain by
Butler & Tanner, Frome, Somerset .

Contents

Dedicated to the late
Colonel J.W. Isaacs MBE TD
1937–87
Co-founder of the Berkshire Yeomanry Museum

Foreword

By Colonel P.M.B. Sutcliffe TD, CBE, DL

In the past there have been many attempts to write an authoritative history of the Berkshire Yeomanry. Many of these have faltered in the making perhaps because the task of research was too daunting, or perhaps because having written it the would-be author found editing and printing too onerous. The work produced in 1950 by Colonel Skrine was a notable effort, but it was with great pleasure that I learned this book was to be published and that I was to have the opportunity to write the foreword.

I shall begin by describing the book as a potted history – and this is not a detriment to the fine work of its three authors. I have seen the wealth of information that, with considerable patience and diligence, the authors have compiled at Windsor. If I say that, in common with many regiments, the war diaries alone would fill a 100-page text book, the reader can get some idea both of the mass of information collected and of the great care which has been exercised in distilling all the available data into this short and definitive history.

The authors, Andrew French, Stuart Sampson and Tony Verey, and their editor, Simon Frost, have all served as Territorials in the Berkshire Yeomanry, the earliest of them since 1968, and between them they share more than eighty years of experience and service; with no doubt many more to come. It is to their credit that they have in both words and deeds done so much to preserve the traditions of the Berkshire Yeomanry.

I make mention of these matters to assure the doubtful reader of the strength of the authors' rightful claim that this history is well researched. This is important because inevitably there are certain gaps in the chronology and, to some, certain surprises, ghosts of the past laid to rest, particularly in relation to the early years. It may be that further more obscure research may bring additional details to life and the authors are continuing their efforts, having in mind the writing of a longer work covering details of many individuals who served with the regiment.

At this point I must digress to thank all those many contributors past and present who have kindly added their treasures to the many items now contained within the Berkshire Yeomanry Museum at Windsor. The current curators, Tony Verey and Andrew French, have brought order out of chaos and consumed much of their own time in cataloguing and revitalizing the displays – the variety and richness of the collection is a constant wonder to me. Those readers who have seen it (and all should do so!) will wish me to pause to honour the memory of the late Colonel Jim Isaacs who, together with WOI Brian Lane, founded the museum in the early 1970s.

The successor unit, the 94 (Berkshire Yeomanry) Signal Squadron, part of 71st Yeomanry Signal Regiment, has retained to this day many of its traditions, particularly in the form of its dress. It is only proper to record that this has happened against the backdrop of pressure for uniformity throughout the army, which has resulted in the loss of many fine traditions and uniforms, particularly of Yeomanry units. The unremitting efforts of honorary colonels, commanding officers and squadron commanders have ensured that all squadrons within the regiment have retained their unique identity. Long may it continue.

To end with I merely exhort the reader to enjoy this book, to admire the many photographs and drawings and to take pride and pleasure in the continuing history of a fine volunteer unit.

The authors and their editor: (left to right) Major W.S. Sampson; Colonel A.P. Verey; Major S.H. Frost; WOII (SSM) A.G. French

Editor's note:

Colonel Sutcliffe was posted to the Berkshire Yeomanry from 121 HAC OCTU in 1942 and served in the UK, India, Malaysia, Java and Burma. As adjutant he was the last man to leave when the regiment was stood down in 1946. He rejoined when the Territorial Army (TA) was reformed and served in one capacity or another for the next forty years. This included service with 345 (Berkshire Yeomanry) Medium Regiment RA TA, and R (Berkshire Yeomanry) Battery of 299 Field Regiment RA TA, and then as Second-in-Command of 299 Field Regiment. In 1961 he was appointed OC of C Squadron Berkshire and Westminster Dragoons and served as acting commanding officer of that regiment during the prolonged absence through ill-health of the then commanding officer, for which he was awarded the MBE.

He raised and commanded the Royal Berkshire Territorials before being promoted colonel, serving at Eastern and South Eastern Headquarters. He was

The regimental badge based on the Uffington white horse. This horse, carved into the chalk hillside above the village of Uffington, is thought to date back to 2000 BC and was adopted as a regimental badge by the Berkshire Yeomanry in 1901

appointed ADC to the Queen in 1970 and Deputy Lieutenant of Hampshire in 1973. He was elected chairman of Eastern Wessex TAVRA in 1975, was chairman of the National Recruiting Committee and vice-chairman of the Council of TAVRAs, retiring in 1984. He was appointed CBE in 1983 and was Honorary Colonel of 94 (Berkshire Yeomanry) Signal Squadron from 1979 to 1988. Active as ever, he farms with his wife Anne, herself a doughty supporter of the TA, at Burntwood in Hampshire.

Annual camp at Medmenham in 1923. 396 Battery (Buckingham-shire and Berkshire Yeomanry) Field Brigade RFA

Acknowledgements

The authors acknowledge with gratitude the following individuals, institutions, museums and trusts who have supplied or assisted with the illustrations, photographs and written material: Aldershot Army Museum; Army Museums' Ogilby Trust; Berkshire Yeomanry Museum; Berkshire Yeomanry Old Comrades Association; British Library; P.H.D. Crichton; DBA Healthcare Communications; D. Dobson; Jim Farrar Photographic; The Flint-Shipman Yeomanry and Volunteer Collection; Miss P. Froom; R.G. Harris; The Illustrated London News; Imperial War Museum; B.P. Lane; Lord Parmoor and the Buckinghamshire Military Museum Trust; Public Records Office; Royal County of Berkshire Cultural Services: Library and Information Service; B. Salter; Staff College, Camberley; R. Treherne.

Winners of the Loyd Lindsay Cup at annual camp at Patcham, 1913. Sergeant Major Seal holds the trophy, with (left to right) Sergeant L. Blyde; Trooper (unnamed); Corporal H. Blyde; Sergeant S. Kerry. The winning section was from B (Reading) Squadron

CHAPTER 1
The First Hundred Years

WARS WITH FRANCE

Yeomanry history begins with the French declaration of war in 1793 upon the monarchies of Europe, when the British Government realized that the regular forces of the Crown would be inadequate to resist a French invasion. A non-regular or volunteer force was advocated and in 1794 Parliament passed an Act which permitted the raising of volunteer corps: the Lord Lieutenant of each county was invited to raise units of both cavalry and infantry. Infantry volunteers were drawn mainly from the ranks of the unskilled workers, while Yeomanry recruits came from the farmers and tradesmen. Yeomanry officers were the gentlemen of the county.

According to the *Reading Mercury* of 21 April 1794 the first mounted troop raised in Berkshire consisted of 'several Gentlemen and respectable tradesmen' of Abingdon who, at a meeting convened by the High Sheriff in that month, offered their services, resolving 'That we are ready and willing at all times to stand forward in a constitutional manner in defence of our King and Country'. They were styled the Abingdon Independent Cavalry and were commanded by Captain Thomas Prince. The conditions and extent of service of the Abingdon Troop were typical for Berkshire: to be ready at the call of His Majesty, the

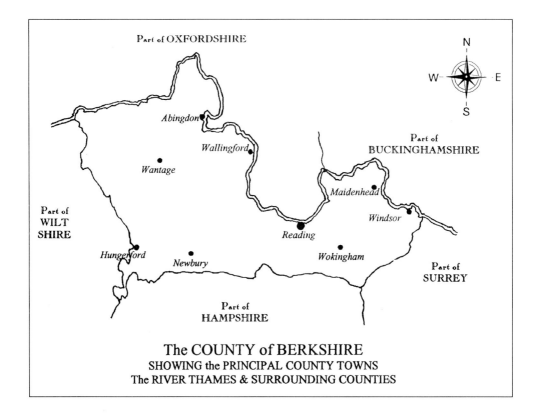

The COUNTY of BERKSHIRE
SHOWING the PRINCIPAL COUNTY TOWNS
The RIVER THAMES & SURROUNDING COUNTIES

Lord Lieutenant or Sheriff for the suppression of riots within five miles of Abingdon and, on the special call of His Majesty, out of the county in case of actual invasion. Typically the training of a troop consisted of one day and one evening drill per week, although this could vary widely depending on the troop and the season of the year. Membership was perforce limited to those who owned a horse and who could absent themselves from their trade, business or farm.

Although from time to time attempts were made in the county to raise other troops, it was not until 1798, with renewed fears of a French invasion, that a second troop of volunteer cavalry was formed. The Woodley Cavalry was commanded by Captain Henry Addington, Speaker of the House of Commons

1789–1801. By June of that year four other mounted troops had been raised, at Newbury, Thatcham, Hungerford and Maidenhead.

In July 1799 the whole of the Berkshire Volunteer Corps, both Yeomanry Cavalry and Infantry, were reviewed by King George III on Bulmarsh Heath, near Reading. The Yeomanry (some 183 horse) were drawn up to form two wings with the infantry in the centre. After performing their different manoeuvres, including sword exercises at full gallop in both attack and defence, they received the royal thanks, His Majesty expressing particular satisfaction with 'the good order, regularity, military appearance . . . of the Volunteer Corps of the County of Berkshire'.

In the absence of a French invasion the Yeomanry only saw action when dealing with civil disturbances. Prior to the establishment in 1855 of the police force in Berkshire the Yeomanry was called out nine times to assist the authorities. The first recorded incident involving the Yeomanry occurred in June 1800 when they were called out by the local magistrate to suppress food riots. Some three to four hundred people had assembled in Thatcham to agitate for an increase in agricultural wages and for the provision of food at a lower price. The Thatcham Troop were alerted, and on the first occasion the crowd dispersed peacefully when confronted by the cavalry, whose appearance rendered it unnecessary for the magistrate to read the Riot Act. The next day a large body assembled at Highclere and were pursued by the Thatcham and Newbury Troops as far as Hurstbourne Tarrant in Hampshire. This time the Riot Act had to be read twice and a detachment of the Newbury Troop under Lieutenant Slocock was sent in to scatter the mob.

INSTRUCTIONS

DESIGNED FOR THE USE OF

OFFICERS,

NON-COMMISSIONED OFFICERS,

AND

PRIVATES,

OF THE

WOODLEY,

AND OTHER

VOLUNTEER CAVALRY,

DEDICATED BY PERMISSION TO

The Right Hon. Henry Addington,

COMMANDING THE WOODLEY CORPS.

BY W. PENNY,

Serjeant Major of the 20th Reg. of Light Dragoons.

[*ENTERED AT STATIONERS HALL.*]

READING:

PRINTED FOR THE AUTHOR,

BY SMART AND COWSLADE, AND SOLD BY ALL OTHER

BOOKSELLERS;

Price to Subscribers, 3s.—Non-Subscribers, 4s.

The frontispiece from a training pamphlet from 1804, a copy of which is held by the Berkshire Yeomanry Museum

In 1800 two further troops were formed in Berkshire, the Wargrave Rangers commanded by Captain Moris Ximines and the Loyal Windsor Cavalry commanded by Captain John Sturges. Both these officers had previously served in the Windsor Foresters (or 5th Regiment of Fencible Cavalry). This regiment, formed for home defence duties in 1794, had been stationed in Edinburgh on garrison duty until its disbandment in 1800.

With the concluding of the Peace of Amiens in 1802 there was a brief respite from the war with France. All troops except those of Abingdon, Woodley and Windsor were disbanded. But when war resumed the following year all the old troops were reformed, together with two new troops, one at Aldermaston and one in the Vale of White Horse. By the end of 1803 Berkshire could field the following Yeomanry Cavalry units:

Troop	*Commanded by:*
Abingdon Yeomanry	Captain E. Child
Woodley Cavalry	Captain H. Addington
Loyal Windsor Cavalry	Captain J. Sturges
Maidenhead Cavalry	Captain W. Payne
Hungerford Yeomanry	Captain J. Pearce
Wargrave Rangers	Captain M. Ximines
Thatcham Volunteer Cavalry	Captain W. Mount
Donnington with Newbury Cavalry	Captain A. Bacon
Aldermaston Cavalry	Captain W. Congreve
Vale of White Horse Cavalry	Captain J. Spicer

In 1804 the Abingdon, Hungerford, Donnington with Newbury and Vale of White Horse Troops were formed into the 1st Regiment of the Berkshire Yeomanry Cavalry under the command of Lieutenant-Colonel Charles Dundas MP. He and his second-in-command, Major F. S. Stead, had held similar posts with the Berkshire Provisional Cavalry, a conscripted militia-type regiment that had served in the West Country during its brief existence from 1797 to 1800. At the outset the 1st Regiment of the Berkshire Yeomanry Cavalry consisted of 16 officers and 199 other ranks. For the few occasions each year that the regiment mustered together the usual rendezvous was the Red House on Wantage Down. In June 1805 King George III again inspected the cavalry and infantry volunteers on Bulmarsh Heath, expressing 'particular gratification in witnessing the military perfection of his Berkshire Volunteers'.

Some detail survives concerning the style of uniform worn in the early days. The choice had much to do with the taste and wealth of individual captains. However, by 1804 the uniform generally consisted of a blue jacket with scarlet facings and shoulder wings with silver lace and cording; officers and quartermasters wore a crimson sash and all ranks wore white breeches, black boots and white crossbelt with black pouch; the helmet was the light dragoon pattern with a black turban and the plume coloured red under white.

In the eastern half of the county regimentation was less well advanced. An attempt was made in 1805 to form the Woodley, Maidenhead, Windsor and Wargrave troops into a second regiment. Although they all came together for permanent duty (as annual camp was then known) at Henley that year, the experiment was not a success, foundering on a lack of agreement over who was to command. In 1814 the Wargrave and Woodley troops joined the 1st Regiment; the other independent

Lieutenant William Hallet
from a painting by
H. Edridge. Lieutenant
Hallet served with
Abingdon Troop 1st
Regiment of Berkshire
Yeomanry Cavalry from
1804 to 1815

troops had by then been disbanded. The Wargrave Troop was disbanded in 1819 leaving the 1st Regiment with five troops on its establishment.

In 1820 William Payne, the former captain of the Maidenhead Troop, raised the Eastern Regiment of Berkshire Yeomanry Cavalry, taking the rank of Major-Commandant. On the 17 July 1821 the Eastern Berkshire Cavalry marched into Windsor, honoured as one of the five Yeomanry Regiments who were chosen to do duty on the occasion of King George IV's coronation. They remained on duty for seven days, returning on the 23 July.

As an example of annual training, in 1826 the Eastern Regiment assembled for eight days on 27 May in Maidenhead, their normal location for annual training. The muster rolls show an attendance of 113 NCOs and men. The *Windsor and Eton Express* of 10 June 1826 reported:

> The Eastern Berkshire Yeomanry completed their term of permanent duty at Maidenhead on Monday last. On the Thursday preceding, the Squadron was inspected by Major Arthur Chichester of the Second Life Guards, when the appearance and admirable condition of the men and horses, and the rapidity and precision with which the various evolutions were performed, called forth the highest praise from the officer. On Sunday the officers and men attended divine service at the new Chapel . . . the members of the corps were most gratified to find that some of the . . . inhabitants had resigned their pews for their accommodation, intending a compliment to the soldier-like and orderly conduct of the men during their stay among them.

DISBANDMENT AND REFORMATION

In December 1827 a Home Office circular was issued disbanding a large number of Yeomanry units, including both regiments of Berkshire Yeomanry. The late 1820s were a period of financial constraint and in an effort to reduce public expenditure the Government was unwilling to maintain Yeomanry units in districts where they had not been called out in aid of the civil power during the previous ten years. Accordingly, the 1st Berkshire Yeomanry Cavalry was disbanded in January 1828, and the Eastern Berkshire Yeomanry Cavalry in April the same year. Arms and accoutrements were handed in and returned to the Ordnance Office and accounts and pay sheets settled.

In 1830 the demands by local labourers both for higher wages and for less reliance on the machinery that had increased unemployment caused riots throughout the country. Berkshire was particularly hard hit and threshing machines were wrecked while barns, haystacks and farmhouses were burnt. The Grenadier Guards were summoned from London and they, along with former members of the Donnington and Newbury troop of Yeomanry, moved off to Kintbury, the centre of disorder. Many rioters were arrested by the Guards who searched the village while it was surrounded by the Yeomanry. Faced with the so-called 'Machine Riots' and the general agitation caused by the Reform Bill that was prevalent throughout the country, the Government had to retreat from its position and expand the Yeomanry force. 'It is vain now,' wrote a Berkshire magistrate, 'to lament the dismissal of the Yeomanry force in this country. If it had existed, all these insurrectionary movements would have been easily controlled.'

In Berkshire four independent troops were raised in 1831, at Hungerford, Welford with Newbury, Woolley (near Wantage and not to be confused with Woodley near Reading), and the Vale of White Horse. During the agricultural riots of 1835–6 in Berkshire these troops were fully employed, detached parties acting as prisoner escorts and such-like.

The following year there were again Government expenditure cuts; in Berkshire three troops were disbanded leaving only the Hungerford Troop in existence. And so it remained for fifteen years. Then, following yet further fears of a French invasion, a second troop was formed in 1852, and a third a year later. These three troops were based at Hungerford, Reading and Newbury. To avoid the threat of disbandment under the Cardwell reforms a fourth troop was raised at Wantage in 1871. At the same time, and for the same reason, the men of the Taplow Lancers (South Bucks Yeomanry) joined the Berkshire Yeomanry's B Troop, which at that time was based at Windsor under the command of Captain Roger Eykyn MP.

During the 1840s the name evolved through usage from the Hungerford Corps of Yeomanry Cavalry to the Royal Berkshire Yeomanry Cavalry. With no record of royal sanction for the Yeomanry, this title properly refers to the county of Royal Berkshire, a title awarded to the County by King George IV.

A new troop was formed in 1890 at Wokingham, replacing that at Hungerford, although the Regimental Headquarters (RHQ) remained based at Hungerford until 1895 when it removed to Reading. A home defence scheme of 1893 paved the way forward with some idea of a proper organization for the Yeomanry and other volunteers. The Berkshire

Trooper Charles Smith, a farmer, of C (Newbury) Troop, photographed in 1895 in full dress (dragoon pattern, scarlet jacket with blue facings, white metal helmet, brass fittings and a white horsehair plume)

Yeomanry were brigaded with the Middlesex Yeomanry to form the 1st Yeomanry Cavalry Brigade. In 1894 they trained under canvas for the first time, and Queen Victoria inspected the assembled troops in Windsor Great Park. In 1895 the Regiment's establishment was two squadrons: the 1st, comprising A (Wokingham) Troop and B (Reading) Troop; and the 2nd, comprising C (Newbury) Troop and D (Wantage) Troop.

CHAPTER 2
Nineteenth-century Weapons and Training

WEAPONS 1794–1899

In the early days, regulations laid down that the yeoman carried a light dragoon sabre with an iron scabbard, and a pair of muzzle-loading pistols in horse holsters. Twelve men in each troop also carried a carbine. For many years the annual ammunition allowance per man was ten rounds of ball and twenty-four rounds of blank together with two flints. In 1848 the 'almost useless flint and steel carbines and pistols', as described by the *Reading Mercury*, were condemned and replaced by the percussion lock carbine. The introduction of ball cartridges obviated the need to ram separate powder, ball and wad down the barrel and was viewed as a great advantage. However, even this carbine was only effective at some 60 yards and it was not until 1871 that a long range weapon was introduced, namely the Westley-Richards 'monkey-tail' carbine. This in turn was replaced ten years later by the Snider breech-loading conversion of the Enfield carbine, which was superseded in 1886 by the Martini-Henry. The .303 Martini-Metford was introduced in 1896.

Examination of illustrations from 1881 reveal that the 1853 cavalry pattern sword was still in use. It was

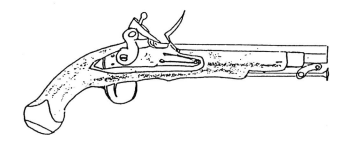

1794 Yeomanry flintlock
holster pistol 16 bore,
15-in long

1892 cavalry carbine,
Martini-Metford .303-in

eventually replaced by the 1882 cavalry pattern sword
which, together with the 1885 scabbard, remained in
service until the Boer War.

ANNUAL CAMP

From early days until 1900 annual camp consisted of
between eight and ten days' training based at one of
the towns of the county. The drill-ground would be a
park or large field adjacent to the town and most days
were spent on mounted drill with the occasional field
day. The artist Richard Caton-Woodville who served
as a private soldier in the Royal Berkshire Yeomanry
Cavalry described his experiences of permanent duty
in 1879 thus:

My first year's training with the regiment was
spent at Hungerford. These were the good old
yeoman days: much fun, little work, and seven and

Trooper in full dress pre-1880: red jacket with blue facings and the old pattern black dragoon helmet

sixpence per day for privates and non-commissioned officers. We rode or hired our own horses, and you could see some valuable animals ridden in the ranks, especially by the real yeoman farmers. We drilled in single rank in those days, and the first two days were always a sore trial for all concerned.

The horses were not accustomed to each other, and there was always a great amount of kicking and bad language. 'Don't talk in the ranks!', was the everlasting cry. The real work of drill was of course in the hands of the sergeant-majors, as most of the officers themselves in those slack days knew next to nothing about it. . . . Our drill started at 10 a.m. and at 1.00 p.m. a pause was made to rest the horses and refresh the men for one hour. At the end of this hour the bugle sounded. . . . Then another two or three hours' drill, and then the march back to quarters. The rest of the evening was spent in singsong at the various inns and hotels where most of the regiment were quartered, or at any rate the various messes were held, while the band discoursed sweet music in front of the officers' mess during the evening, and late at night the men made the town unsafe and noisy.

At first we were still armed with the old Westley-Richards carbine – you had to insert a paper cartridge, place a cap on the nipple, and once out of three the flash of the cap didn't pierce the cartridge. It was curious how familiarly the yeomen spoke to the officers. One day at 'advance dismounted in skirmishing order,' a yeoman was ordered to call out, 'Here, Captain, can you lend us a corkscrew? I have got a cork in my carbine and can't get it out.' The sergeant-majors were also very original in their instructions. At sword exercise, for instance, you heard, 'Now then, men, when I say 'draw', you don't draw, but when I say 'sudds', you whips 'em out right smart!'

TRAINING

On training in the early 1870s Colonel G.C. Ricardo, who was later to command the regiment, had this to say:

> I have myself seen once when the colonel was not out at the training, another officer in command, . . . pull a bit of paper out of his holster pipe and read the drill through. Most weird movements they were. 'Change front three-quarters right back, on the third squadron', was a sample. This took at least ten minutes to perform, it was done very solemnly, at a walk, of course, and as every troop leader had to give some different word of command, very few gave a right one. We all looked over our shoulders and asked our sergeant-major for the proper word, so it naturally took time.
>
> Then far too much time was wasted in marching past – outpost work was only practised once in the eight days' training, so it naturally follows that the force was not strong at it.

The officers of the Berkshire Yeomanry at Newbury in 1884. (From left to right, standing) Surgeon R.H. Barker; Lieutenant E.P. Crowdy; Lieutenant R.W. Cosier; Captain G.C. Ricardo; Captain M.J.A. Eyre; Lieutenant H.E. Rhodes; Lieutenant C.E. Pigott; Lieutenant G.O. Sloper; Captain H.M.A. Warde (19th Hussars, adjutant). (Seated) Captain W.H. Dunn; Lieutenant-Colonel G.S. Willes; Major the Hon. O.W. Craven; Captain J. Hargreaves

Then the old system of billeting the men in towns was never a good one. Men brought their own grooms, or rather one man looked after three Yeomen's horses – the actual rider never saw his horse from the time he got off him in the afternoon 'til he got on his back again the next morning; he never put on his own tackle, never knew whether his horse had ever been fed, or what sort of food he required; all he knew was, that if he was blown up by this captain for some irregularity of putting on, or cleanliness of kit, it was his man's fault. His one ambition was to have a good week, and as a rule he had it.

I must say . . . that however badly the men had been doing on the day previous, no matter whether the day was fine or wet, they always

Permanent staff, *c.* 1890. (From left to right) Sergeant-Majors Burr, Robinson, Roach and Smith

pulled themselves together on the inspection day, and did their best for the credit of the regiment. The talking was appreciably less, and they one and all tried to help the officers. What used to strike the inspecting officer more than anything, was that the men drilled well enough for all intents and purposes, but the constant chatter . . . used to make him wonder how it was the work was done at all. Now, I am happy to say, this is a thing of the past.

The old officers' mess used to be as expensive as it was possible to be – it was held at the principal hotel in the town. Officers invited half the county to dinner, drank champagne by the bucketful, had big gambles, or else jovial spirits would paint the town red – this, I am happy to say, has quite gone out

Mounted parade in full dress, Northbrook Street, Newbury 1897, on the occasion of Queen Victoria's diamond jubilee

owing to the advent of camp life and its proper discipline. This also means that an officer's mess bill is very slight compared with what it used to be; whisky and soda has taken the place of champagne, and the county is only invited to the regimental sports.

Sergeant Rooke, *c*. 1895. Note the crown worn above the rank stripes in the style of the Lifeguards to denote the rank of sergeant

By all accounts the standard of training improved in the 1880s and 1890s as this extract from the *Regimental Journal* of 1895 shows:

The Berkshire Yeomanry band, *c.* 1898

The officers of the Berkshire Yeomanry at Reading in 1890. A break for refreshment on the Maiden Erleigh estate during annual camp

The Reading Troop on parade, *c.* 1898, in Station Road, Reading

On Monday, 20th May, the Squadrons paraded independently under their respective leaders (the 1st or 'A' Squadron commanded by Captain E.D. Stern, in Drill order; and the 2nd or 'B' Squadron led by Captain the Earl of Craven, in Drill order, with helmets but without plumes) for outpost and reconnaissance duties; sealed instructions were handed to each commander by the Brigade Adjutant. Blank ammunition was issued to troops, and a detailed report of the day's work was to be handed in by 5 p.m. The 1st Squadron marched to Tidmarsh, and from there started at 10 a.m. to fight its way into Reading, in opposition to the 2nd Squadron, who formed a chain of outposts across the line of advance, having its left on the Bath road in Reading, the reserve at Tilehurst behind the Common, and the right on the

Annual camp 1894, in Windsor Great Park

Pangbourne and Reading road. The 1st Squadron were unable to force the position held by the 2nd Squadron, and the decision of the umpires was in favour of the defending Squadron. Lieutenant-Colonel the Hon. O.W. Craven, Major G.C. Ricardo and the Brigade Adjutant being the umpires.

The pre-1901 regimental badge, worn on the dragoon helmet. The Star and Crescent are derived from the Coat of Arms of the Borough of Hungerford

CHAPTER 3

The Boer War and its Aftermath

THE BOER WAR

Within two months of the outbreak of war in October 1899 it had become clear that the British Army faced an uphill task if the Boers, expert marksmen and acknowledged horsemen, were to be defeated. After the disasters of 'Black Week' in early December the Government sanctioned the formation of the Imperial Yeomanry, the first contingent of which sailed to South Africa in the first quarter of 1900. Along with men from Canada, Australia and New Zealand, the Imperial Yeomanry provided a large proportion of the force of mounted infantry (that is, riflemen who could cover large distances fairly rapidly and who could undertake the traditional roles of light cavalry, scouting and patrolling).

The Berkshire Yeomanry had sufficient volunteers to form two companies, the 39th Company of the 10th Battalion Imperial Yeomanry and the 58th Company of the 15th Battalion. After an inspection by HRH the Prince of Wales at Lords cricket ground the 39th Company (nicknamed the 'dirty ninth') commanded by Major Ricardo sailed for South Africa in the SS *Norman* on 10 February 1900. The arrival of the first contingent occurred at the beginning of the two year guerrilla phase of the war. After marching to

Kimberley their first encounter with the enemy was at Boshof on 5 April 1900 against a party of Boers commanded by a Frenchman, General de Villebois Moreuil, who was fatally wounded in the action.

The Berkshires joined the main advance to Pretoria under Lord Roberts and then moved to the Orange Free State. At this stage of the war there were no set-piece battles. Campaigning consisted of constant patrolling, escort duties and hunting the small parties of Boers who were a constant menace. The unsuccessful attempt to relieve the Irish Yeomanry at Lindley at the end of May was the first major operation in which the battalion took part. Thereafter the 10th Battalion joined Lord Methuen's force hunting Christian de Wet,

Private H. Tudor Crosthwaite, stockbroker, 39th (Berkshire) Company, photographed in 1900 at Vryburg, serving in Lord Methuen's force during the campaign against de Wet

one of the ablest of the Boer leaders, whose band numbered some 2,600. Although the chase was ultimately unsuccessful, in that de Wet escaped into the Transvaal, the continual harassment by the British troops prevented him from inflicting any great damage. H. Tudor Crosthwaite, a stockbroker serving in the ranks of the 39th Company, in a letter dated 30 August describes one operation:

Members of the 39th (Berkshire) Company in South Africa in the summer of 1900. A few moments' rest

> On the Sunday we had a long running fight which resulted in our taking one gun and enabling some 60 British prisoners to escape; they were riding on an ox wagon in the Boer convoy when a good shot from our 15 pounder caught the oxen and stopped progress. The Boer guard fled and Tommy Atkins rushed like a hare to us. . . . Off again in a few hours

and for the next few days we seemed to do nothing but march – alternately walking and riding all through the day and night with very few hours to rest and feed. It was very funny seeing men fast asleep rolling about in their saddles and at each halt men were on the ground and asleep in five seconds.

The 58th Company performed similar duties although details of its operations are sparse. It is known that they departed Cape Town on 1 May 1900, taking only the supplies and kit that would fit on their saddles, and moved up-country to Kimberley. Thereafter they moved off with the rest of the 15th Battalion to Boshof and then joined Lord Methuen's column moving through

Private Kennet Mason, 39th (Berkshire) Company 10th Battalion Imperial Yeomanry, photographed (bottom left) in khaki uniform in 1900 before departing for South Africa, and later (bottom right) in Mafeking after a few months' hard campaigning. After his return Mason became the landlord of the Railway Hotel at Mortimer, near Reading

Lindley, Bethlehem, Heilbron, Harrismith and Kroonstadt.

The first contingent of Imperial Yeomanry had enlisted for one year only and because no recruiting was allowed to replace casualties it was necessary to raise a second contingent in early 1901. Because the new units were formed from several sources it is not possible to identify any single unit with the Berkshire Yeomanry. A third contingent raised in 1902 did not reach South Africa until after the end of the war.

1901–1913

The British Army learnt many lessons from the Boer War, which later enabled the country to enter the Great War properly equipped and trained. The Yeomanry came out of the Boer War with a greatly enhanced reputation and, more importantly, with a proper role. Ever since the end of the Crimean War in 1856 there had been considerable debate as to the proper use to be made of the Volunteers. The need for Yeomanry had been particularly weakened by the establishment of proper police forces and the transition from a rural to an urban economy. Eventually the War Office identified a requirement for mounted soldiers who could shoot well and fight on foot as well as move quickly over long distances. This was something which the Yeomanry had proved that they could do.

The war had revealed a serious flaw in the Army's ability to fight a major war overseas without proper reserves. The various Volunteer and Militia units, including the Yeomanry, were not available for overseas service and the various units formed during the war had to be created from volunteers. The Haldane reforms of 1907, which created the Territorial Force, were designed

Four Yeomen from B (Reading) Squadron at annual camp at Churn, *c.* 1904, wearing khaki uniform with red facings and slouch hats. On the far right is trooper Bill Froom, a farmer from Mortimer

Officers at annual camp at Churn in 1908. (From left to right, standing) 2nd Lieutenant C.J.G.T. Walmesley; Lieutenant R.M. Hughes; 2nd Lieutenant A.T. West; Lieutenant the Hon. H.G. Henderson; Captain J.T. Wigan (Adjutant); Captain J.L. Nickisson; Captain The Marquis of Downshire; Lieutenant the Hon. A.P. Henderson; Lieutenant R.M. Pearson; Lieutenant G.M. Wilder; (seated) an officer of the Berkshire RHA; Captain E.S. Gooch; Major E.A. Barry; Colonel G.C. Ricardo (commanding); Major J.P.B. Karslake, Major E.R. Portal, Captain E.M. Slaughter, Captain and Quartermaster W.L. Rose; (front row) 2nd Lieutenant Blackall G.P. Simmonds; 2nd Lieutenant W.E.G. Niven; 2nd Lieutenant P.M.N. Wroughton; Lieutenant F.G. Strange; 2nd Lieutenant E.T.T. Drake; 2nd Lieutenant the Hon. E.B. Henderson; 2nd Lieutenant E.B.G. Foster

to overcome this difficulty. The Berkshire Yeomanry was to find itself within the Territorial Force, an integral part of the nation's defences incorporating more formalized links with the Regular Army. As with other counties the administration of the regiment came under the County Territorial Association presided over by the Lord Lieutenant whose continuing role as overseer of the military forces in the county was thus maintained.

Captain The Marquis of Downshire commanding a mounted guard of Berkshire Yeomen in No. 1 dress (blue with red facings) in Windsor, *c.* 1909

In 1901 the regiment received the title of the Berkshire Imperial Yeomanry and by 1902 had adopted khaki uniform; blue patrols replaced the scarlet full dress. At this time the regiment was formed into four squadrons: A (Windsor) Squadron, B (Reading) Squadron, C (Newbury) Squadron and D (Wantage) Squadron. In 1907 the Regimental Headquarters was established at Yeomanry House,

A (Windsor) Squadron on parade, *c.* 1912

The signal section with their equipment at annual camp at Churn in 1912. Regimental Sergeant-Major
E. Seal is seated on the right. Clearly visible are the signalling lamps, spotting telescopes and flags

The machine-gun section during annual camp at Patcham on the South Downs near Brighton in 1913. Squadron Sergeant-Major W. Cox is in the centre foreground

Reading. The Berkshire Yeomanry was brigaded with the Royal Bucks Hussars and the Queen's Own Oxfordshire Hussars, the whole forming the 2nd South Midland Brigade.

It is clear from photographs and written accounts that the regiment trained to a high standard. The regular location for annual camp was at Churn by the Ridgeway on the Berkshire Downs, a good base for all sorts of cavalry manoeuvres. The Lee-Metford rifle had been introduced after the Boer War and training included rifle firing on the range at Churn. Although the sword was formally withdrawn, sword drill still continued. A further example of the advanced approach of the British Army of this period is shown by the provision at Regimental Headquarters of both machine-gun and signalling sections.

A fine example of the khaki uniform of 1913, complete with bandolier and rifle in leather butt bucket. This is Lance-Corporal L.H. Beard, Hungerford Troop C (Newbury) Squadron

CHAPTER 4

The Great War – Mobilization and Gallipoli

MOBILIZATION

Although war had been anticipated for some time and preparations were well advanced, its outbreak came suddenly. Within days of the announcement of mobilization at the beginning of August 1914 the Berkshire Yeomanry was shaking down at Churn, while the Regimental Depot at Yeomanry House, Reading, dealt with an influx of volunteers. Part of the mobilization plan was that the regiment should be reorganized into three squadrons; C (Newbury) Squadron was disbanded and its manpower redistributed within the regiment.

GALLIPOLI, 1915

Like many other Yeomanry regiments the Berkshire Yeomanry at first remained in the United Kingdom on home defence duties. On mobilization the Oxfordshire Hussars had joined the British Expeditionary Force in France and Flanders and their place in the brigade was taken by the Dorsetshire Yeomanry. In April 1915 the division, complete with horses, was sent with other troops to Egypt where they remained until ordered to the Dardanelles in August. Although training in the

Middle East had been as mounted troops, the decision was made in early August that the Yeomanry would fight dismounted; each regiment fielded a double-strength squadron, leaving the horses with a strong rear party. The brigade (or regiment as it was now officially and confusingly called because of its diminished size) sailed from Alexandria on 14 August aboard SS *Lake Michigan*; after transhipment on the 17th at Mudros the

Preparations for war in Great Knollys Street, Reading, in August 1914

regiment landed on A Beach East at Suvla on the morning of the 18th.

CHOCOLATE HILL (HILL 53) AND SCIMITAR HILL (HILL 70)

The regiment's first contact with the Turks was a bloody affair. The brigade war diary records:

20th August 8.00 p.m. The brigade marched by night to Lala Baba and bivouacked on the shore west of the hill (rate of march about one mile per hour owing to frequent halts to allow supply carts to pass both ways).

21st August 3.00 p.m. The brigade took part in general attack against enemy entrenched in Hill 70.

Second Troop B (Reading) Squadron, commanded by 2nd Lieutenant C.B. Krabbe, at Churn in 1914. Private F.W.O. Potts (later to win the VC) is fourth from the left in the back row. Troop Sergeant H.C. Blyde, sitting on Krabbe's right, was commissioned in 1915 and later won the MC at Gallipoli

The brigade advanced across the open, leaving the Salt Lake on the left flank, by regiments in following order: Berks, Dorsets, Bucks, each regiment in line of troop columns. Machine guns brigaded on right flank. During this advance the brigade came under heavy shrapnel fire (casualties in this advance two officers, forty other ranks).

The Berkshire Yeomanry escorting Turkish prisoners through the streets of Cairo in the summer of 1915

4.45 p.m. The brigade formed up under cover of Hill 53.

5.00 p.m. Verbal orders received to attack Hill 70.

5.15 p.m. Berkshire Yeomanry started the attack. Dorsets, Bucks following in support. During this

Stores coming ashore on the beach at Suvla Bay

41

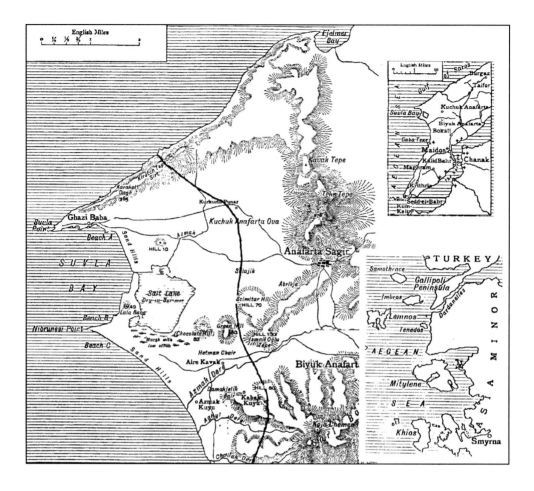

attack heavy casualties were caused in all regiments – owing to the skilful way in which the enemy's trenches had been sited it was impossible to see them (a large amount of scrub which had been burnt made the advance difficult). The Dorsets and Bucks had meanwhile reinforced the Berks first line and also prolonged their left.

6.15 p.m. The Berks with a portion of the Bucks and Dorsets charged and captured the enemy's front trench. The portion captured formed the apex of a triangle and owing to enfilade fire the Brigade

Gallipoli area of operations. The solid line represents the final British and ANZAC positions prior to withdrawal

was unable to hold the trench and had to evacuate it. All brigade staff and 70% regimental officers had become casualties.

8.00 p.m. The brigade gradually retired in various small parties and eventually rallied on 22nd on western slope of Hill 53.

R. Caton-Woodville's engraving of the Berkshire Yeomanry attacking Turkish positions on Scimitar Hill (Hill 70) on 21 August 1915

The following strengths	Going into action		Returned	
	Officers	Other Ranks	Officers	Other Ranks
HQ and Signal Troop	4	47	0	45
Bucks	9	312	3	178
Dorsets	8	301	1	159
Berks	9	314	4	150

Included among the Berkshire officers killed were the Commanding Officer, Major E.S. Gooch and Lieutenant W.E.G. Niven, the father of the actor

In the trenches above Suvla Bay. The Berkshire Yeomanry lived this way for three months, dining mostly on MacConachie stew and plum & apple jam

David Niven. A Victoria Cross, two Military Crosses, three Distinguished Conduct Medals and eight Mentions in Despatches were won by soldiers of the Berkshire Yeomanry on this occasion. The Victoria Cross was the first awarded to the Yeomanry in the war.

PRIVATE F.W.O. POTTS VC

The first report of this man's valour was:

31st Infantry Brigade

I have pleasure in bringing to your notice an act of conspicuous bravery and devotion by No. 1300 Pte Potts F.W.O. of the Berkshire Yeomanry, 2nd Mounted Division, who, though himself wounded in the thigh and buttocks in the attack on Hill 70 on 21st August 1915 after lying out for over 48 hours under the Turkish trenches succeeded in fixing a shovel to the equipment of his comrade Pte Arthur Andrews of the same Corps, who was severely wounded in the groin, and dragging himself across 600 yards of ground to within a short distance of our lines though fired on by the Turkish trench, reaching our line at about 9.30 p.m. on the 23rd instant. Pte Potts remained beside his comrade during the 48 hours, though he could himself have reached the trenches during that period.

Witnesses: Capt R. H. Scott
No. 11290 Sgt W. Brown
No. 12854 L/Cpl E. Crawlee
All 6th Regiment Innis Fus
31st Infantry Brigade

Private F.W.O. Potts VC

WITHDRAWAL

For the remaining three months of the Gallipoli
campaign the regiment remained in defence on and
around Chocolate Hill, plagued by heat, disease, lack
of shade and water, and the continuous shell and rifle
fire of the Turks. On 1 November 1915 the 2nd
Mounted Division finally embarked for Mudros and
Egypt. The evacuation from Gallipoli was the only
well-executed part of a disastrous campaign.

The Great War:
Mediterranean and
Middle Eastern Theatres
of War

CHAPTER 5

The Great War – Egypt and Palestine

EGYPT

Of the 135 Berkshire Yeomen who had remained behind with the horses in Cairo, a number went with the composite Yeomanry Regiment which was part of the force sent to Salonika. This operation on the border between Greece and Bulgaria lasted until 1918 but very little concerning the Berkshire Yeomanry's role there has been recorded.

In Egypt, however, although the main Turkish threat to the Suez Canal and the British troops in Egypt came from the East, attacks were also made on their rear by the Senussi; this fanatical sect had been plaguing the French and Italians since 1900. In December 1915 the Western Frontier Force was formed, which included the 2nd Composite Yeomanry Regiment containing a squadron each of Berkshire, Dorset and Buckinghamshire Yeomanry, with the aim of eliminating the Senussi attacks. On 11 December a detached force of armoured cars and horsemen including elements of the Berkshire Yeomanry successfully attacked an enemy party of about four hundred at Wadi Senab; there was a similar action two days later at Em El Rakhum. This force was led by Major Wigan who had been wounded at Gallipoli while in temporary

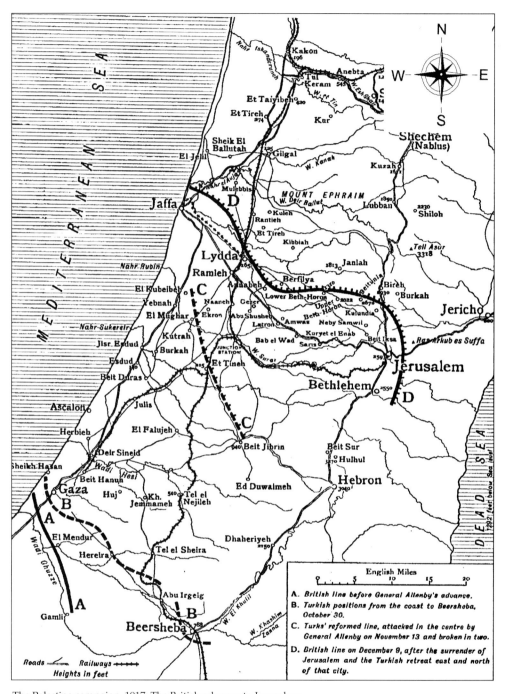

The Palestine campaign, 1917. The British advance to Jerusalem

command of the regiment. Heavy rains over Christmas delayed further operations until mid-January when the force was able to drive the Senussi out of Hazazin.

Patrolling the desert in Upper Egypt, 1916

After this action the Yeomanry was again reorganized. The 2nd Composite Yeomanry Regiment was broken up and the various squadrons were reunited with the survivors from Gallipoli. The 2nd South Midland Mounted Brigade was renumbered the 6th Mounted Brigade. Some months later the Camel Corps was raised as part of the Western Frontier Force and many yeomen swapped horse for camel.

Action against the Senussi was resumed in the Western desert in February 1916 and on the 25th of that month a charge by the Dorset Yeomanry was

decisive in breaking up the Senussi forces who never again stood up to the British.

During the summer and autumn of 1916 the Berkshire Yeomanry were employed in patrolling and outpost duties in Upper Egypt. Then under the command of Lieutenant-Colonel J.T. Wigan, they moved east to the Suez Canal where the defences were extended into the Sinai. There was little action during the remainder of the year for the Berkshire Yeomanry who, as a result, were occupied with patrolling and training.

Some of A Squadron's officers resting on the way to Nekhl in the Sinai, January 1917. (Left to right) Lieutenant H.C. Blyde; 2nd Lieutenant A.H.K. Williams; Major G.M. Wilder; Lieutenant D.W. Tooth

THE BATTLES FOR GAZA

In January 1917 the British began their advance towards Jerusalem. After dislodging the Turks from the Sinai the British column advanced towards the enemy's principal strong point at Gaza, arriving there in early March. The First Battle of Gaza (26/27 March) was not a success. Fog delayed the infantry attack on what turned out to be well prepared positions and the enemy were able to bring up reinforcements to repel the attack. The Berkshire Yeomanry formed part of the screening force that was attacked by four thousand Turks who arrived from Huj; although they were held off their arrival caused the British commander to order his force to retire. The Berkshires withdrew successfully but by then had lost their commanding officer, Lieutenant-Colonel J.T. Wigan, who had been seriously wounded.

The Second Battle of Gaza was fought from 17–19 April, with the main assault planned for the 19th. The Imperial Mounted Division was ordered to mount a diversionary dismounted attack. After a strong Turkish counter-attack the 6th Mounted Brigade, held in reserve, was called up: they advanced at the gallop. Eyewitness Lieutenant O. Teichman (veterinary officer of the Worcestershire Yeomanry), later writing in the *Cavalry Journal* of 1936, described the action thus:

> The situation of the Worcestershire Yeomanry, indeed of the 5th Mounted Brigade was very critical when an urgent message was sent to the 6th Mounted Brigade. Looking south-westwards from the Atawineh Ridge across two miles of level ground towards the Wadi Munkheileh, the writer could see the latter enveloped in clouds of black smoke from the shells which were bursting over it. Suddenly he saw a sight which thrilled him: out of

Major Philip Wroughton, commanding D Squadron, was killed in action in the Second Battle of Gaza, 1917. An outstanding officer much mourned by the regiment, his memorial stands on the Berkshire Downs at Woolley. A wreath is laid there annually to this day

An officer of the Royal Berkshire Yeomanry in 1807 (*Edwards, 1896*)
Inset: A Royal Berkshire Yeomanry officer in full dress, 1898

Newly adopted uniforms in 1907, from the original artwork produced for Gale and Polden regimental postcard series

Top: A team from the Royal Berkshire Yeomanry Cavalry compete in the Loyd Lindsay Cup on Wimbledon Common in 1885 (*R. Caton-Woodville, 1885*)

Bottom: The charge of the 6th Mounted Brigade at El Mughar during the British advance on Jerusalem, 13 November 1917. The Berks, Bucks and Dorset Yeomanry were ordered to capture the Turkish position after the infantry had been held up through lack of cover. Their dashing charge drove out the enemy *(from an original painting by J.P. Beadle)*

Left: Lieutenant-Colonel the Hon. G.W.N. Palmer commanded 345 (Berkshire Yeomanry) Medium Regiment RA (TA) from 1954 to 1956. He later became Lord Lieutenant of Berkshire

Below: Berkshire Yeomanry 25-pounders on Sennybridge Ranges in the mid-1950s

Bottom: Exercise 'Red Shoes', a two-week communication exercise, took place on Longmoor Training Area during annual camp, October 1978

Top: The Austin K9 1-ton, D11/R234 radio vehicle of 885 Troop on exercise in 1975

Bottom: Squadron command post troop with a ¾-ton FFR Land Rover, an Austin K9 1-ton office truck and a ½-ton Land Rover line truck, Longmoor Training Area, 1982

Top: The Guidon Party at Longmoor in October 1990

Bottom: Squadron Headquarters at annual camp at Longmoor in 1984. Standing (left to right) Corporal R. Burns; Corporal A.G. French; Lance-Corporal P. Leng; Corporal C. Dunk; Signalman K. Rank; Signalman T. Bark; Corporal W.A. Walker; Lance-Corporal N. McNevin; Signalman M. Archer. (Seated) Captain A.G.C. Adams; 2nd-Lieutenant W.S. Sampson; WO2 (SSM) J.R. Stewart; Major A.P. Verey TD; Captain L. Graham; WO2 M. Stubbs; SSgt A. Reynolds

Left: The Berkshire Yeomanry guidon and escort take part in the march-past in front of HM The Queen at the 200th anniversary of the Yeomanry in Windsor Great Park, 17 April 1994

Below: Led by Major W.S. Sampson and Squadron Sergeant-Major A.G. French, the squadron march past the Guildhall, Windsor, on the occasion of the granting of the Freedom of the Royal Borough of Windsor and Maidenhead, 23 April 1994

Above: HM The Queen inspects representative troops and guidons of the Yeomanry Regiments at the Royal Review in Windsor Great Park, 17 April 1994. The Berkshire guidon is on the left of the line

Top: The original design of the Guidon of the Abingdon Troop from Messrs Hawke's pattern book of 1794

Bottom: The present Guidon of the Berkshire Yeomanry. Of crimson silk damask, it measures 2ft 8in in depth and 3ft 5in to the points of the swallow tails, and is embroidered and fringed with gold. It was refurbished in 1990 with funds generously provided by old comrades

the wall of smoke which hid Munkheileh there emerged a mass of horsemen which gradually opened out into extended order and filled the foreground. It was the Berkshire Yeomanry led by their CO Lt Col J.T. Wigan, and C Sqdn Bucks Yeo. Disdaining to dismount, for they knew it was only a matter of minutes, the yeomanry galloped on, here and there a horse and rider coming down as they covered the two miles between Munkheileh and the Atawineh Ridge. Dismounting, the yeomanry came into action at once and after driving in the first lines of the Turkish advance, they effectively re-established the broken line.

The Berkshire Yeomanry captured a number of the enemy trenches and fought off further Turkish attacks. Major Philip Wroughton, much loved by all ranks, was fatally wounded by shellfire during the battle. Subsequently, as in the first battle, the British troops were ordered to withdraw.

After the failure of Second Gaza, General Sir Edmund Allenby assumed command of the British Forces. A cavalryman and one of the best British generals of the Great War he reorganized his forces before resuming the advance on Jerusalem. The Desert Mounted Corps was reformed to provide three cavalry divisions: the Yeomanry Mounted Division, the Australian Mounted Division and the ANZAC Mounted Division. The task of these three cavalry divisions during the build-up was to patrol the waterless expanses between the two opposing armies. As one division patrolled, another was held in support while the third went into training camp.

THE ADVANCE TO JERUSALEM

The Third Battle of Gaza took place at the beginning of November 1917; the Berkshire Yeomanry was engaged in minor actions near Beersheba, part of the successful covering operation aimed at preventing counter-attacks similar to those that had bedevilled the earlier battles. The result of the battle was to drive the Turks from the Gaza–Beersheba line and the British forces moved on in pursuit of the enemy.

EL MUGHAR, 13 NOVEMBER 1917

El Mughar ridge, held in strength by the Turks, dominated the surrounding countryside. The 6th Mounted Brigade was ordered to dislodge the enemy. The Bucks and Dorsets led the advance, covering four thousand yards at the gallop under heavy machine-gun fire, and took the enemy trenches at the charge. The Turks began a heavy fire from the flank and it was not until the Berkshires arrived that the Turks were finally driven off the ridge. In all, the brigade captured one thousand prisoners, two field guns and fourteen machine guns. This action, in which the Turks lost several hundred dead, is cited in the Official History as a fine example of the successful employment of all arms. The artillery attached to the 6th Mounted Brigade throughout this campaign was the Berkshire Battery RHA, another Territorial unit.

The Yeomanry had a similar success two days later when the Yeomanry Mounted Division was ordered to take the Abu Shusheh ridge, held by a strong Turkish rearguard. A and D Squadrons of the

Berkshires attacked dismounted on the left towards the highest point of the ridge, while B Squadron, with the Bucks Yeomanry, made a mounted assault on the lower slopes to the right, with the Dorsets in reserve. This combination of mounted and dismounted attacks proved entirely successful, with the Turks losing 750 men for the loss on the British side of 50.

The operations in Palestine formed part of the last great cavalry campaign. In his history of the campaign, Field Marshal Lord Wavell cited the charge at El Mughar as one of the 'notable demonstrations of the dictum that "speed is armour" and shows that, provided there is no natural obstacle to stop it, a mounted attack may get

Soldiers from the Berkshire Section of the 17th Brigade Machine-Gun Squadron, equipped with the Vickers machine-gun, on outpost duty in Palestine, 1917. Machine-guns and limbers were carried by pack-horse

Pack-horses of the Machine-Gun Squadron resting and feeding, January 1917

Turkish machine-gunners, Palestine 1917. Their water-cooled machine-guns were similar to the British Vickers

home by sheer speed where an infantry attack would be slow and costly'.

After a few days' rest and reorganization the Yeomanry Mounted Division marched into the Judaean Hills. Advance parties found the enemy well dug in on the Zeitoun ridge. For two days there was desperate fighting among the rocks and ravines in atrocious weather. Sadly, in the afternoon of the second day, the Berkshire Yeomanry commanding officer, Lieutenant-Colonel A.M. Pirie, was killed. The arrival of Turkish reinforcements led to a British withdrawal leaving just a precarious foothold on the ridge. The Turks mounted an attack on 27 November 1917. The Zeitoun outpost, held by the Berkshires (numbering three officers and sixty men), was bravely defended all afternoon.

A battery of Turkish artillery and gunners, Palestine 1917. Much of the Turkish artillery was crewed by Austrian gunners. Guns like these were charged by the Warwickshire and Worcestershire Yeomanry Regiments on 8 November 1917 during the Third Battle of Gaza and successfully taken, despite many casualties

Reinforcements arrived at night but the order to withdraw came the next day when there remained only twenty soldiers still able to fight, under Lieutenant L.N. Sutton. The Turkish attack was finally beaten off and the greatly reduced 6th Mounted Brigade withdrew from the front line for the last time on 30 November 1917.

CHAPTER 6

The Great War – France and Flanders

CONVERSION TO MACHINE-GUN CORPS

By January 1918 the Berkshire Yeomanry was brought up to a strength of 20 officers and 450 other ranks and resumed training and refitting. In April the Berkshire Yeomanry was amalgamated with the Royal Bucks Hussars under Lieutenant-Colonel F.H. Cripps to form the 101st Battalion, Machine-Gun Corps. Like heavy artillery, machine-gun battalions were corps troops under the direct command of the corps commander. In an attack their role was to provide covering fire for the infantry during their initial assault. Thereafter, the individual companies supported the brigades as needed. Flexibility was the principal requirement, coupled with the ability to master the detailed staff requirements of the complex fire-plans, all of which was ideally suited to the Yeomanry tradition and spirit.

In May 1918 the battalion was ordered to France. The fighting on the Western Front had reached a critical stage; the French forces had taken the brunt of the German offensive of March 1918, and the American troops were still in training.

The journey began inauspiciously; within hours of leaving on the night of 26 May the SS *Leasowe*

Army Order No. 416 dated 22 October 1915 authorized the formation of the Machine-Gun Corps. Its strength comprised 6,427 officers and 123,835 other ranks, and its casualties totalled 62,049 (including 12,498 killed). The corps was awarded twelve Victoria Crosses. In the Book of Remembrance of the Machine-Gun Corps it is recorded that: 'They received an unexampled number of awards for gallantry and self-sacrifice far beyond the call of duty'. The corps was disbanded in 1922

Lieutenant-Colonel the Hon. F.H. Cripps DSO, Commanding Officer 101st Battalion, Machine-Gun
Corps. He commanded the amalgamated battalion of Buckinghamshire and Berkshire Yeomanry
following their conversion to Machine-Gun Corps in the spring of 1918. Described by his adjutant as a
leader-elan, Fred Cripps was the brother of the Labour politician Sir Stafford Cripps

Castle was torpedoed with the loss of the adjutant and one soldier, both drowned. There was a three week delay while lost equipment was replaced. After re-embarkation on HMT *Caledonia* the regiment landed at Taranto in Italy on the 21 June and entrained for France, arriving in time to take part in the final allied offensive which began on 8 August 1918.

The battalion saw their first action in support of the 51st Highland Division in the Battle of Scarpe on 29 August. The fighting was in complete contrast to that in Palestine – the dash across the desert on horseback was now replaced by slow, deliberate assault across muddy fields and shell-holes.

On 16 September the battalion moved to Belgium in preparation for the attack on Wytschaete Ridge south

SS *Leasowe Castle* in Alexandria Harbour, 26 May 1918

of Ypres. This attack began on 28 September and the
battalion's task was to support the 35th and 14th
Divisions in the assault on the Comines Canal. In
contrast to many of the Great War attacks there was
no preliminary artillery bombardment and the
machine-gunners went forward with the leading
waves of infantry. The attack was successful and the
battalion remained with the 35th Division for their
last action of the war, at Tieghem on the 31 October
1918, which resulted in the easily accomplished
capture of the western bank of the Schelde. Plans
to cross the river on the 11 November were brought
forward after the Germans withdrew on the 8th. The
101st battalion, no longer required for the assault,
was back in Courtrai when the Armistice was
announced on the 11th, and there it remained until
demobilization a few months later.

Berkshire Yeomanry
survivors from the
SS *Leasowe Castle*,
torpedoed by a German
U-boat, photographed on
board one of the rescue
ships, 27 May 1918

2/1ST AND 3/1ST BERKSHIRE YEOMANRY

In 1914 all Territorial Force regiments had been ordered to form second line units. As well as acting in a home defence role they provided a source of trained soldiers for the first line regiment. In addition to the regiment deployed to the Middle East, designated 1/1st, the Berkshire Yeomanry formed two further regiments.

The 2/1st Berkshire Yeomanry was raised on 23 September 1914 and formed at Bearwood, Wokingham, where it remained until May 1915 when it moved, after a month at Churn, to Kings Lynn in Norfolk. East Anglia was believed to be the likely site for a German invasion and although this threat never materialized the enemy carried out several air raids in the area. The war diary for 1915–1916 records 2/1st Berkshire Yeomanry as providing 'observations posts for hostile aircraft', as well as taking part in the occasional general turnout when the German navy came close to the coast. At the end of March 1916 horses were exchanged for bicycles. Mounted thus, 2/1st remained in England until early 1918 when they were sent to Ireland to carry out garrison and guard duties.

The 3/1st Berkshire Yeomanry was raised at Bearwood in April 1915 as a training unit for the first and second line regiments. It remained in existence until the spring of 1917 when training within the British Army was reorganized. From July 1915 the 3/1st was based at Tidworth although between October 1915 and April 1916 its headquarters were based at Windsor in the new drill hall in the High Street.

RECRUITING DURING THE GREAT WAR

Until conscription was introduced in 1917 recruiting was the responsibility of the county associations.

No. 2649 Private Lewis
J. Salter, 3/1st Berkshire
Yeomanry, in a splendid
studio photograph taken
in 1915. Private Salter was
later posted to 1/1st
Berkshire Yeomanry and
saw action in Gallipoli,
Egypt and Palestine
where he was wounded in
the 2nd Battle of Gaza.
After the war Lewis Salter
became a publican

After the first burst of enthusiasm in 1914 those recruiting figures that survive reveal a considerable variation from month to month. In August and September 1914 1/1st Berks Yeomanry received some 190 volunteers. 2/1st Berks Yeomanry raised 431 recruits between September and December 1914. A further 92 recruits were raised between January 1915 and September 1916, 53 of whom were recruited within the Kings Lynn district. 3/1st Berkshire Yeomanry recruited 491 men in 1915 and more than 200 in 1916. By the middle of January 1917, 800 men had passed through 3/1st Berkshire Yeomanry as follows:

Posting:	1/1st Berks Yeomanry	461	Others:	Discharged	46
	Machine-Gun Corps	18		Commissioned	12
	Other Units (incl. 2/1st)	114		Deserted	3
	BEF France (4th Royal Berks)	131		Died	2
	Army Reserve	13			

CHAPTER 7

Between the Wars 1919–39

After the 'war to end all wars' there was a lull before the Territorial Army began training again. For the Yeomanry the role of cavalry was greatly reduced; only the fourteen senior regiments remained as such. The majority became gunners and, in that role, were able to retain their horses for a few more years.

For the Berkshire Yeomanry the first post-war camp, held in 1921, was their last as cavalry. At that camp they were shown their new weapon, the 18-pounder field gun. From 1922 to 1939 the Berkshire Yeomanry provided two batteries (395, initially from Windsor and Reading, and 396, Newbury and Hungerford) of 99th (Buckinghamshire and Berkshire Yeomanry) Field Brigade RFA.

At first recruiting was slow but it gradually picked up as the regiment built up expertise in its new role. Like all other parts of the public service at that time financial stringency was severe (the 1932 annual camp for the Territorial Army was axed) and re-equipment was slow. In 1927 the draught horses were replaced by quaint Fordson tractors; these in turn were superseded the following year by civilian Morris lorries which were to last until past 1939. During this period training carried on in much the same way: a gunnery practice camp was held in alternate years at Okehampton, Bulford or

Annual camp,
Medmenham, 1923

Westdown. In the intervening years camps were held either locally at Medmenham or Hurley, or at the seaside, for example, at Budleigh Salterton or Corfe Castle. Drill nights were not held between camp and Christmas, but once a week between Christmas and Easter, and thereafter twice weekly until camp. Weekend training was minimal; social occasions were frequent.

The pace of life was enviably relaxed as this extract from Colonel Skrine's history shows. 'As the Regiment became more experienced in later years it was not felt really necessary to hold Battery Commander's conference more than once a year. It was usually held in April in the Cavalry Club. The

Annual camp, Medmenham, 1923. 'The first week at camp was always a rodeo . . . usually resolved in finding two or three teams that would go!' (Lieutenant-Colonel Skrine)

Commanding Officer and Adjutant would meet more frequently, perhaps once a month, generally at the Ritz Grill'. By 1933 the regiment was sufficiently trained to exercise as a whole; thereafter refinements such as tactical concealment, night exercises and wireless training followed on.

A particular honour was bestowed on the Berkshire Yeomanry in 1937, to mark the coronation of King George VI, when 395 Battery was chosen to fire the salute in Windsor Great Park, a rare privilege for the Territorial Army.

Bringing the guns into action at annual camp, Medmenham in 1923

In 1938, following the Munich Crisis, 99th (Buckinghamshire and Berkshire Yeomanry) Field Brigade RFA was reorganized and reduced from four batteries, each of two troops, to two batteries, each of three troops. Berkshire provided three troops of four guns each, based at Newbury, Wantage and Windsor; the Hungerford and Reading sections were closed. Between camps in 1938 and 1939 the regiment was retitled 99th (Buckinghamshire and Berkshire Yeomanry) Field Regiment RA TA. Early in 1939 when preparations for conscription were under way, service in the Territorial Army was introduced as an

396 Battery at annual camp, Hurley, in 1927, now equipped with Fordson tractors to tow the 18-pounders and limbers

396 Battery, commanded by Major Hugh Crosland, at annual camp at Hurley in 1927

Annual camp at Budleigh Salterton in 1938; 18-pounders drawn up for inspection

alternative to compulsory call-up. 99th (Buckingham-shire and Berkshire Yeomanry) Field Regiment RA TA was divided to provide two full regiments, 99th (Buckinghamshire Yeomanry) Field Regiment RA TA and 145th (Berkshire Yeomanry) Field Regiment RA (TA).

A gun-drill competition with an 18-pounder drawn by a Fordson tractor at annual camp at Hurley in 1927

CHAPTER 8

The Second World War

MOBILIZATION AND HOME DEFENCE

At the outbreak of war, 145 (Berkshire Yeomanry) Regiment RA TA, under command of Lieutenant-Colonel W.H. Crosland, mobilized in its several drill halls and on 10 September 1939 moved to Newbury racecourse. Most of its equipment had gone to its sister unit, the Buckinghamshire Yeomanry, who were assigned to the BEF and therefore had priority. Training was only achieved at all thanks to the unselfish assistance of the 1st and 3rd Brigades RHA based at Aldershot. The surroundings were somewhat eccentric, as illustrated by the following extract from Sir William Mount's 396 Battery orders: 'HQ and D Troops will occupy Tattersall Lunch Room. E and F Troops will occupy Tattersall Champagne Bar. 396 Battery Office will be the Press Room.'

In February 1940 the regiment moved out to local villages, including Kingston Bagpuize, and the surrounding countryside, where they undertook air sentry duties and anti-parachute patrols, particularly along the Berkshire ridgeway. The invasion of Holland in May 1940 emphasized the importance of these activities. In addition a mobile battery group was formed, commanded by Major Sir William Mount Bt, and dispatched to Bognor Regis on the south coast under the command of 4th Division.

NORTHERN IRELAND

After Dunkirk one of the perceived German invasion routes was through Eire. To their considerable surprise the 61st Division, commanded by Major-General Carton de Wiart, and which included the Berkshire Yeomanry, found themselves ordered to move to Northern Ireland to reinforce the defences against any possible enemy moves in that direction. The regiment arrived at Bangor in July 1940. Between that date and January 1942 the regiment was based in several locations in Northern Ireland: after six weeks in Bangor there was a move to Antrim where they remained until the summer of 1941. The next stay, at Moneymore, was shorter, preceding a move in January 1942 to Newton Stewart from where, in May,

Training for war: a gunnery demonstration in Wantage in 1939

Gunners Ernie King and Claud Hine with Bombardier Bishop ready for guard duty at the Hop Huts, Kingston Bagpuize, autumn 1939

The Mobile Troop in early 1940 practising deployment drills under the watchful eye of BSM Tickle (left). The vehicle is a brewer's dray which could not tow the gun; instead it had to be manhandled on and off the dray

Dismounting drills, 1940. Gunner Keen is at the rear

the regiment was divided between Londonderry and Coleraine.

Throughout this period the regiment remained in support of 183 Infantry Brigade. Each battery was associated with an infantry battalion: 395 Battery with the 10th Battalion Worcestershire Regiment; 396 Battery with 5th Battalion Gloucestershire Regiment; and 509 Battery with the 5th Northamptonshire Regiment. The brigade anti-tank regiment was provided by the Oxfordshire Yeomanry.

Lieutenant-Colonel Skrine wrote thus:

Before we left, the worthy people of Bangor had their first taste of war. The SS *Troutpool* was mined at the entrance to Belfast Lough and lay half

Gunners Day and Sines, with an unnamed pickaxe wielder, of Mobile Battery, under the command of Major Sir William Mount, digging in at Bognor, June 1940

Camouflaged gun position, Northern Ireland, 1941

Brewing up on exercise, Northern Ireland, 1942

Major D.A. Campbell,
current Chairman of the
Old Comrades'
Association, seen here on
exercise in Northern
Ireland, 1942

submerged in shallow water two miles off shore. A
small detachment, led by John Puxley, were soon in
a boat making for the ship to see what could be
salved! Thus early did they practise the art of
combined operations and conservation of supplies.
They brought back some useful items, including
small-arms ammunition, but were discouraged
from making a further search by an armed naval
detachment from Belfast who had come to resist
boarders.

Soon after the regiment's arrival in Northern Ireland equipment began to arrive in quantity and gunnery training intensified. In September 1940 came French 75s which were a useful addition to the regiment's 18-pounders and 4.5-in howitzers. However, this did mean that a battery such as 396 had three troops each equipped with a different gun requiring its own particular drills. Not that this mattered over much as there was no ammunition for any of the guns. Later came the renowned 25-pounder. Anti-tank training figured large in the programme and the Sperrin Mountains were often used as a training area.

Lieutenant-Colonel Skrine was later to write:

No account of the stay in Northern Ireland could be complete without some reference to the

A 'universal carrier' on exercise, Northern Ireland, 1942, with Bombardier Barlow and Lance-Bombardier White (right of picture)

wonderful boon for those granted forty-eight hours leave to visit Eire. If they could afford it, people generally went to Dublin, to begin with, where there was lots of good food, wine and, best of all, lights everywhere. The moral effect of no blackout was astonishing. They could arrive in their bedrooms after dark, rush to the windows and fling open the curtains, letting all the light of O'Connell Street come flooding into the room. Then there was Leopardstown, Nass or Navan, or wherever it might be. The whole thing was a wonderful tonic. Nearly everybody would bring back a tiny bit of contraband, of course, and there were some remarkable 'customs' stories, into which we need not go, but by and large people played the game and there was never any attempt at smuggling on a big scale.

The regiment returned to England from Northern Ireland in 1943. Pictured here, they had stopped for lunch at Kendal on the journey south during the move to Southend-on-Sea

In February 1943 the regiment moved back to the mainland, first to Southend-on-Sea, and from there via Beaconsfield in April, and Aylesbury in July, to Eastry, Kent in November 1943. It was during this period that the regiment learnt – with great disappointment – that despite their acknowledged high standard of training they were not to be included in the order of battle for the Normandy invasion. Instead they found themselves part of the deception plan called Operation 'Fortitude', intended to convince the Germans that the invasion would come from Kent to the Pas de Calais. After this phase the batteries ran marshalling camps for the Allied invasion forces. At this stage officers and

Captain A. Nicholson (second from left) in charge of an Observation Post (OP) Party on exercise 'somewhere in England' in the summer of 1943

soldiers were lost through being posted as reinforcements to other units already in France. Deeply concerned about the state of affairs the commanding officer, through the proper channels, requested and was allowed to make an appeal direct to the Crown.

Exercise 'Spartan' in 1943 was an important part of the preparations for D-Day

THE FAR EAST

Perhaps as a result of this appeal the regiment found itself at last on its way overseas in an operational role. On 18 November 1944 the Berkshire Yeomanry received orders to prepare to move overseas to a tropical climate. Leaving East Grinstead in two special trains they embarked at Liverpool on 29 January 1945, arriving in India on 23 February. The regiment moved

(Left to right) Captain M. England, Captain R. Lewis and Captain J. Puxley during Exercise 'Spartan', 1943

The Far East (*Times* New
Mercator projection)

to Dehra Dun where from March 1945 509 Battery
acted as the demonstration unit at the tactical training
centre while the other two batteries provided live
firing practice for the infantry battalions, a process
called 'battle inoculation'.

The end of the war in Europe was marked by
celebrations in New Delhi in mid-May 1945. The
Newbury Battery (396) had the honour of firing the
victory salute, while 395 Battery formed part of the
procession.

Towards the end of June 1945 the regiment moved

to Poona from where, after a short stay, it went to Bangalore. Training continued in preparation for the invasion of Malaya (codenamed Operation 'Zipper'). However, before the operation could be mounted, the Japanese government surrendered as a result of the dropping of atomic bombs on Hiroshima and Nagasaki. Nevertheless, some fifteen days later the invasion went ahead on the assumption that it would be an opposed landing. It was not known whether the Japanese would follow their government's instructions to surrender. The regiment landed at Morib beaches on 9 September and, in fact, opposition was non-existent as the Japanese had withdrawn inland. Although some difficulties were experienced with sand bars and muddy beaches the regiment was soon ashore and harbouring at Morib airfield. By 19 September the

Well-laden transports approach Morib beach during Operation 'Zipper' in Malaya, August 1945

Officers' mess, Malaya, 1945

The landings at Morib beach

Disarming surrendering Japanese officers at Ipoh, September 1945

regiment had taken up garrison duties at Ipoh where they assisted in maintaining law and order. Particular trouble was experienced with looters and in dealing with large numbers of surrendering Japanese soldiers.

Victory parade salute at Ipoh, 30 September 1945

JAVA

Indonesia, then the Dutch East Indies, was in turmoil. Following the Japanese surrender there was no effective government and a full scale insurrection was in progress against the resumption of Dutch rule. The nationalist army which had been trained by the

Japanese but which was under the effective control of the nationalist leader, Sukarno, numbered some 120,000 men. In Sourabaya alone there were 12,000 armed men. 49th Indian Infantry Brigade, which had only recently landed at Sourabaya, had lost 18 officers and 374 soldiers in bitter fighting while attempting to restore order. Many civilians, Dutch, Chinese and others, had been massacred.

The regiment, under the command of Lieutenant-Colonel R.L.T. Burges, later awarded the DSO for his leadership in this operation, was dispatched in support of 5th Indian Division to Java, sailing from

Loading in Singapore prior to sailing for Indonesia, December 1945

Singapore aboard HMS *Queen Emma* on 1 December. On 5 December, within hours of their arrival at Sourabaya, 509 Battery were in action in support of a mobile infantry column successfully engaging a number of targets. Next day 395 Battery were also undertaking similar operations with another column. Scarcely a day passed until early April without two of the three batteries being in action. Enemy tactics included sniping, blowing up bridges, laying mines and setting ambushes. A few incidents from Lieutenant-Colonel W.H. Skrine's history of the campaign illustrate the type of action undertaken:

Guns in action on the road outside Sourabaya, 21 December 1945. They were part of a composite column from 9th Indian Infantry Brigade advancing towards Sidoardjo

In such close country, nearly every kampong [village] by the roadside could be used for an ambush, and some losses from these were inevitable. It is sad to record that, on 18 January,

when a Gurkha patrol was returning to harbour after reconnoitring Krijan with two tanks, a shot was fired at our OP party, killing Sergeant Painter and one of the Gurkhas. Painter was a popular and most efficient signals instructor and was greatly missed in 395 Battery.

Bombardier Pringle operating a 19 set (high frequency radio) in the back of a Willys jeep during the Java campaign

On 10 January there had been much extremist activity on the north side of the perimeter at the village of Mengaute. D Troop guns supporting the 2nd Battalion of the 1st Punjab Regiment were in action early next morning from a position just west of the village. The Punjabis very soon made contact with a party of 25 Indonesians in Brinkang, not far away. They drove them out and found three dead bodies.

The CO of the Punjabis moved his tactical headquarters and two platoons forward to this place soon afterwards. Major Hugh Whitcombe (OC 396 Battery) was with him. This party waited near Brinkang until forward patrols had cleared the kampongs which lay some distance away, to south, west, and north. The CO intended to move north, through Domas, as soon as this place was reported clear.

The leading patrol was first opposed by three medium machine guns firing from a large kampong 3,000 yards west of Brinkang. The patrol cleared this locality, captured one of the machine guns and from there proceeded to clear the settlements to the west and north-west of Domas. Small parties of enemy could be seen withdrawing northwards as the Indians approached.

One of the two platoons at Brinkang now went forward to join the leading patrol in pursuit on the far side of Domas. There was no opposition in this village and the road now seemed to be clear for the remaining platoon and CO's party to follow by the direct road north from Brinkang. While this group was moving forward it was caught in a road block, cleverly concealed and covered by a medium machine gun and about thirty snipers. The

Berkshire Yeomanry 25-pounder in action against the nationalist terrorists during the Sourabaya campaign, Java 1946

extremists held their fire until this HQ party was at very close range. The battalion commander, Lieutenant-Colonel Saljit Singh Kalha, in the leading jeep, was killed outright.

Major Whitcombe was in the second jeep. Hugh was wounded in the first burst of fire and died soon afterwards. The battalion wireless sets were put out of action by small-arms fire and this isolated column lost touch with the other groups. The platoon, under Subedar Karim Khan, took up a defensive position and beat back four attacks by the Indonesians – attacks that went on for an hour and a half. The subedar was awarded a Military Cross for his gallantry in this action. Major Whitcombe's signaller, Lance-Bombardier Gerbaldi, did extremely well; he was wounded at the same time as the CO but stayed on his set until it was shot to pieces and he managed to get back a report of what was happening, together with a very accurate location, which enabled reinforcements to be sent. He was awarded the Military Medal.

For the next few months there followed a number of short sharp battles which saw the regiment in action many times in support of, among others, 9th Indian Infantry Brigade, 23rd Indian Infantry Brigade and 9th Gurkha Rifles. The enemy were well armed and determined, but by April most of the opposition had been overcome. As with subsequent Indonesian campaigns this was extremely successful but little publicized. The regiment provided essential artillery support throughout, firing a total of some twenty thousand rounds and suffering a number of casualties. Two troop commanders, Lieutenants Jimmy Searson and

Raising the white horse flag at Sourabaya

Paul Mathews were mentioned in despatches for their actions in this campaign.

Towards the end of April 1946 the regiment handed over its guns to the Dutch military authorities and by May 1946 the regiment had been disbanded and the majority of its members were en route back to the United Kingdom.

CHAPTER 9

1947 to the Present

Cap badge, Royal
Artillery

ROYAL ARTILLERY 1947–1960

After the war the regiment re-formed (in 1947) as 345
(Berkshire Yeomanry) Medium Regiment RA (TA)
commanded by Lieutenant-Colonel M.L. Wroughton
based at Newbury, and 346 (Berkshire Yeomanry)
Medium Regiment RA (TA) commanded by
Lieutenant-Colonel W.H. Skrine based at Windsor.
Later these two units combined to form one regiment
under the title of 345, commanded by Lieutenant-
Colonel D. Campbell and subsequently by
Lieutenant-Colonel the Hon. G.W.N. Palmer, with its
two batteries in these two towns. In 1957 this
regiment became part of the 299th Field Regiment RA
(TA), formed by amalgamation with the Royal Bucks
Hussars and the Queen's Own Oxfordshire Hussars;
the surviving elements of the Berkshire Yeomanry

formed R Battery. During this period the regiment was variously equipped with 25-pounders, 4.5-in and 5.5-in Medium guns and training, including live firing at annual camp, took place at various locations throughout the UK including Sennybridge and Salisbury Plain.

In 1953 the regiment was honoured with the duty of firing a salute in Windsor Great Park on the occasion of the coronation of Her Majesty Queen Elizabeth. The regiment took delivery at short notice of a number of 25-pounders and worked hard on the necessary gun drills.

ROYAL ARMOURED CORPS 1961–1967

Early in 1961 the Berkshire Yeomanry regained its cavalry role. Through amalgamation with the Westminster Dragoons, they formed the Berkshire and Westminster Dragoons RAC (TA). This armoured car regiment had its C (Berkshire Yeomanry) Squadron based at Windsor and Newbury. They were equipped with Saladin and Daimler armoured cars, of which the latter were soon phased out and replaced by the Ferret scout car. The squadron was commanded by Major P.M.B. Sutcliffe and then by Major R.D. Black. Annual camp took them to places as far afield as Omagh, Lulworth and Bellerby. The regiment provided a number of 'ever readies' who assisted the regular army in Aden during the troubles of the mid-1960s. C Squadron's drill hall at Windsor was relocated to a new building in Bolton Road that was opened by the Duke of Gloucester in May 1964. The Berkshire and Westminster Dragoons provided a mounted guidon party for the occasion. In September 1966 a

Cap badge, Berkshire and Westminster Dragoons RAC (TA)

C Squadron, Berkshire and Westminster Dragoons on exercise, in the early 1960s

Windsor Troop of C Squadron, Berkshire and Westminster Dragoons, in the early 1960s

new guidon was presented to the regiment by Field-Marshal the Earl Alexander of Tunis at the Duke of York's Headquarters, Chelsea.

INFANTRY 1967–1969

In 1967 the Territorial Army was reorganized into the Territorial and Army Volunteer Reserve. Headquarter Squadron of the Berkshire and Westminster Dragoons became Headquarter (Berkshire and Westminster Dragoons) Squadron, Royal Yeomanry Regiment, at Elverton Street, Westminster. The Berkshire Squadron, C Squadron, changed its role, becoming infantry in TAVR category III with the new title of A (Berkshire Yeomanry) Company, Royal Berkshire Territorials. This regiment was an amalgam of the Berkshire Yeomanry, the Royal Berkshire Regiment, gunners and others, and was commanded by Lieutenant-Colonel P.M.B. Sutcliffe.

This was a lean and difficult period for the Berkshire Yeomanry. Much training was carried out unpaid, with the soldiers even contributing to the cost of food and petrol. Even so, the Berkshire Yeomanry Company at Windsor commanded by Major R.D. Black, ably assisted by Company Sergeant-Major B. Lane, continued to train and recruit in its new role.

The cap badge of the Royal Berkshire Territorials and the officers' collar badge of A Company. The backing to the cap badge was a red oval

Corporal Duigenan and members of A (Berks Yeo) Company undergoing anti-tank weapon training on the ranges in the summer of 1968

ROYAL SIGNALS 1969 TO PRESENT

In April 1969 following a further reorganization, all TAVR III units were disbanded and the Berkshire Yeomanry re-formed as 94 (Berkshire Yeomanry) Signal Squadron. As such it was to be part of a composite Yeomanry Signal Regiment whose other three squadrons were found by the Inns of Court and City Yeomanry, the Essex Yeomanry, and the Kent and County of London Yeomanry. It was in recognition of their strong Yeomanry tradition that the regiment was retitled 71 (Yeomanry) Signal Regiment in 1975. The squadron's current role is to provide home defence communications for formation HQs in the UK.

At the start of this period the Berkshire Yeomanry Signal Squadron TA Centres were at Reading, Windsor and Southampton. However, in March 1971 squadron headquarters and the troop based at Reading moved out to join the troop at Windsor. From early 1975 until October 1976 there were two

Cap badge, Royal Corps of Signals

additional troops at Brighton and in March 1977 a
past Berkshire Yeomanry association with Chertsey
was rekindled with the reopening of the TA Centre
there. In 1992, after 'Options for change' the troop at
Southampton was re-roled as Royal Engineers and a
new Berkshire Yeomanry troop was raised at Brock
Barracks, Reading.

As part of the celebrations to mark the 200th
anniversary of the founding of the Yeomanry the
squadron and old comrades took part in the Royal
Review of the Yeomanry held on 17 April 1994 in
Windsor Great Park. Her Majesty Queen Elizabeth II,
Her Majesty Queen Elizabeth the Queen Mother and
His Royal Highness the Duke of Edinburgh attended
the review and the Berkshire Yeomanry were

Annual camp at Burniston
Barracks, Scarborough,
September 1970. Captain
J.R. Stevens (left) with his
Reading-based AFHQ
troop seen here deploying
the generator-powered
Larkspur D11 HF radio
mounted in an Austin K9
1-ton radio vehicle. This
radio was the backbone of
the regiment's
communication system

particularly honoured in leading the line of the
Yeomanry Guidons on to the parade.

On 24 April 1994, at a ceremony in Windsor, the
squadron was honoured by the granting of the
Freedom of the Royal Borough of Windsor and
Maidenhead to mark the long association between the
Berkshire Yeomanry and the Royal Borough. The
occasion was celebrated by a parade through Windsor
town centre, with the salute taken by His Worshipful
the Mayor, Councillor M.A. Scott, followed by a grand
luncheon in the Guildhall.

At the time of writing the squadron is about to
receive new communications equipment. It is well
recruited with 12 officers and 140 soldiers.

Appendix: Units and Commanding Officers

INDEPENDENT TROOPS OF YEOMANRY CAVALRY
Between 1794 and 1804, eleven independent Yeomanry Cavalry Troops were established in Berkshire.

Abingdon Troop	Captain Thomas Prince	1794–1799
	Captain Edward Child	1799–1804
Reading Troop	Captain John Blagrave	1794–1804
Hungerford Troop	Captain John Pearce	1798–1804
Maidenhead Cavalry	Captain William Payne	1798–1804
Newbury Troop	Captain Richard Townsend	1798–1804
Thatcham Cavalry	Captain Commandant John Croft	1798
Wargrave Rangers	Captain Moris Ximines	1798
Woodley Cavalry	Captain Henry Addington MP	1798–1807
Windsor Troop	Captain John Sturges	1800–1807
Vale of White Horse Cavalry	Captain C. Dundas MP/ Captain J. Spicer	1803–1804
Aldermaston Cavalry	Captain William Congreve	1803

FIRST REGIMENT OF BERKSHIRE YEOMANRY CAVALRY
1804–1828   Lieutenant-Colonel C. Dundas MP

EASTERN REGIMENT OF BERKSHIRE YEOMANRY CAVALRY
1820–1828   Major Commandant W. Payne

HUNGERFORD TROOP OF BERKSHIRE YEOMANRY CAVALRY
1831–1834   Captain G. H. Cherry
1834–1839   Captain J. W. Deans Dundas MP
1839–1844   Captain W. Honeywood
1844–1853   Captain G. Willes

ROYAL BERKSHIRE YEOMANRY CAVALRY
1853–1862   Major G. Willes (promoted Lieutenant-Colonel 1862)
1862–1875   Major W. Honeywood (promoted Lieutenant-Colonel 1863)
1875–1894   Lieutenant-Colonel G.S. Willes
1894–1901   Lieutenant-Colonel the Hon. O.W. Craven

BERKSHIRE IMPERIAL YEOMANRY
1901–1904   Lieutenant-Colonel the Hon. O.W. Craven
1904–1908   Lieutenant-Colonel G.C. Ricardo

BERKSHIRE YEOMANRY (TF)
1908–1910	Lieutenant-Colonel G.C. Ricardo
1910–1914	Lieutenant-Colonel Sir E.A. Barry Bt
1914	Lieutenant-Colonel J.B.P. Karslake TD

1/1ST BERKSHIRE YEOMANRY
1914–1915	Lieutenant-Colonel the Hon. H.G. Henderson MP
1915	Lieutenant-Colonel R.M. Hughes
1915–1917	Lieutenant-Colonel J.T. Wigan DSO
1917	Lieutenant-Colonel A.M. Pirie DSO (21st Lancers)
1917–1918	Lieutenant-Colonel Sir R. St J. Gore (Westminster Dragoons)

101 (BUCKINGHAMSHIRE & BERKSHIRE YEOMANRY) BATTALION MACHINE-GUN CORPS
1918–1919	Lieutenant-Colonel the Hon. F.H. Cripps DSO MC (Bucks Yeomanry)

2/1ST BERKSHIRE YEOMANRY
1914–1916	Lieutenant-Colonel J.P.B. Karslake TD
1916–*c.* 1917	Lieutenant-Colonel L.E. Kennard (15th Hussars)
c. 1917–1918	Lieutenant-Colonel P. Moir-Byres (Scottish Horse)
1918–1919	Lieutenant-Colonel G.M. Wilder

3/1ST BERKSHIRE YEOMANRY
1915–1917	Major the Hon. A.P. Henderson

BERKSHIRE YEOMANRY (TA)
1920–1921	Lieutenant-Colonel C.T.J.G. Walmesley DSO MC TD

99TH (BUCKINGHAMSHIRE & BERKSHIRE YEOMANRY) FIELD BRIGADE RA (TA)
1921–1924	Lieutenant-Colonel the Hon. D. Forbes (Royal Artillery)
1924–1929	Lieutenant-Colonel C.T.J.G. Walmesley DSO MC TD
1929–1933	Lieutenant-Colonel E.F. Lawson DSO MC TD (Bucks Yeomanry)
1933–1938	Lieutenant-Colonel H.P. Crosland OBE MC TD DL

99TH (BUCKINGHAMSHIRE & BERKSHIRE YEOMANRY) FIELD REGIMENT RA (TA)
1938–1939	Lieutenant-Colonel W.H. Crosland TD

145TH (BERKSHIRE YEOMANRY) FIELD REGIMENT RA (TA)
1939–1942	Lieutenant-Colonel W.H. Crosland TD
1942–1943	Lieutenant-Colonel E.H. Jackson RA
1943–1945	Lieutenant-Colonel M.L. Wroughton TD
1945–1946	Lieutenant-Colonel R.L.T. Burges DSO RA

345 (BERKSHIRE YEOMANRY) MEDIUM REGIMENT RA (TA)
1947–1951	Lieutenant-Colonel M.L. Wroughton OBE TD
1951–1954	Lieutenant-Colonel D.A. Campbell OBE TD
1954–1956	Lieutenant-Colonel the Hon. G.W.N. Palmer MBE TD

346 (BERKSHIRE YEOMANRY) MEDIUM REGIMENT RA (TA)
1947–1951	Lieutenant-Colonel W.H. Skrine

R (BERKSHIRE YEOMANRY) BATTERY, 299 FIELD REGIMENT RA (TA)
1956–1957   Major P.H.D. Crichton TD
1957–1959   Major P.M.B. Sutcliffe TD
1959–1960   Major J.P.L. Puxley TD

C SQUADRON, BERKSHIRE & WESTMINSTER DRAGOONS RAC (TA)
1961–1964   Major P.M.B. Sutcliffe TD
1964–1967   Major R.D. Black

A (BERKSHIRE YEOMANRY) COMPANY, ROYAL BERKSHIRE
TERRITORIALS
1967–1968   Major R.D. Black

94 (BERKSHIRE YEOMANRY) SIGNAL SQUADRON
1969–1970   Major R.H. Eyton
1970–1972   Major F.K. Bailey TD
1972–1976   Major J.W. Isaacs TD
1976–1980   Major J.R. Stevens TD
1980–1985   Major A.P. Verey TD
1985–1989   Major S.H. Frost TD
1989–1992   Major R.K. Wilkinson TD
1992–1994   Major W.S. Sampson TD
1994–Date   Major G.S. Hornsby

SQUADRON HONORARY COLONELS
1983–1988   Colonel P.M.B. Sutcliffe CBE TD DL
1988–Date   Colonel Sir David Black Bt

Index